Stitch by Stitch

Elizabeth Hobbs Keckly Sews Her Way to Freedom

Text in italics is from **Behind the Scenes, or, Thirty Years a Slave, and Four Years in the White House** *by Elizabeth Keckley.*

Note: Keckly is sometimes spelled Keckley.

Stitch by Stitch

Elizabeth Hobbs Keckly

Sews Her Way to Freedom

by
Connie Schofield-Morrison

Illustrated by
Elizabeth Zunon

HOLIDAY HOUSE · NEW YORK

Elizabeth Hobbs Keckly was born in
February 1818. She wrote in her autobiography,

*My life has been an eventful one. I was born a slave—was
the child of slave parents—therefore I came upon the
earth free in God-like thought, but fettered in action.*

My birthplace was Dinwiddie Court-House, in Virginia.

Lizzy's father was George Pleasant Hobbs. Her mother's name was Agnes, and she was known as Aggy.

5

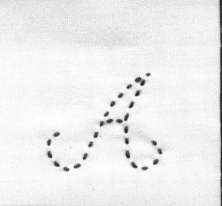

Lizzy and her mother
were the property of
Armistead Burwell.
Lizzy's mother was
a seamstress for
the entire Burwell
household. Though
the law forbade
enslaved persons
to be educated,
Aggy knew how to
read and write.
Lizzy also learned
to read and write.
And she learned
how to sew . . .

stitch by stitch.

1

2

3

4

Lizzy remembered being put to work at the age of four. She was taking care of the Burwell baby when the baby fell out of her cradle. Lizzy was severely beaten.

Later, Lizzy, like her mother, became a seamstress.

My mother was kind and forbearing; . . . and as mother had so much work to do in making clothes, etc., for the family, besides the slaves, I determined to render her all the assistance in my power.

Lizzy helped her mother . . .

stitch by stitch.

At about the age of seven, Lizzy witnessed the auction of an enslaved child, Little Joe, the cook's son.

Master had just purchased his hogs for the winter for which he was unable to pay in full. [Little Joe] came in with a bright face, was placed in the scales, and was sold, like the hogs, at so much per pound.

[His mother] was whipped for grieving for her lost boy. Burwell never liked to see one of his slaves wear a sorrowful face, and those who offended in this particular way were always punished. Alas! The sunny face of the slave is not always an indication of the sunshine in the heart.

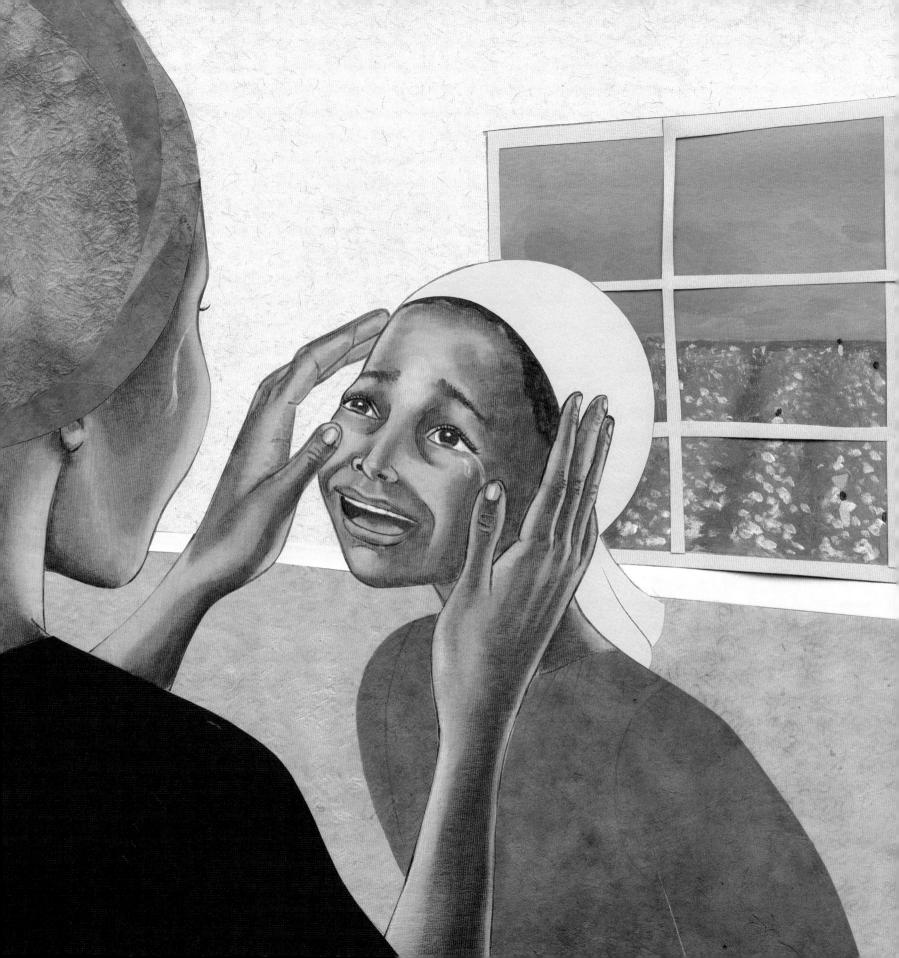

Though Lizzy worked hard, she came under much criticism from Burwell.

I grew strong and healthy, and notwithstanding I knit socks and attended to various kinds of work, I was repeatedly told, when even fourteen years old, that I would never be worth my salt.

Lizzy knitted socks . . .

stitch by stitch.

Soon after Armistead Burwell sent
her to live with his eldest son,
Robert, and Robert's wife, Anna.

I was their only servant. . . .
From the very first I did the
work of three servants and
yet I was scolded and
regarded with mistrust.

While living with Robert and Anna Burwell,
Lizzy was brutally beaten.

Eventually, Lizzy was sent to live with Robert's
sister, Ann Burwell Garland, and her husband,
Hugh Garland, first in Virginia and then in St. Louis,
Missouri. By that time, Lizzy had a son. Mr. Garland
was poor, so Lizzy offered to look for work to support
his family.

*I was fortunate in obtaining work, and in a short
time, I had acquired something of a reputation
as a seamstress and dressmaker. The best ladies
in St. Louis were my patrons, and when my
reputation was once established, I never lacked
for orders. With my needle, I kept bread in the
mouths of seventeen persons for
two years and five months.*

Stitch by stitch.

17

Today, most women buy dresses from a store or online. The dresses are made by designers, patternmakers, cutters, machine operators, and finishers. Hundreds of dresses in dozens of sizes are made in each style.

But when Lizzy lived, a dressmaker would drape a cloth on a patron's body and use the cloth to make a pattern. Either the dressmaker or the patron would buy fabric and trimmings. Then the dressmaker would sew the dress. Each dress was one-of-a-kind and required many hours of work.

St. Louis was a city with communities of free African Americans. While Lizzy lived there, her desire for freedom grew. She made the request to Mr. Garland.

I made a proposition to buy myself and my son. The proposition was bluntly declined, and I was commanded never to broach the subject again. I would not be put off thus, for hope pointed to a freer, brighter life in the future. Why should my son be held in slavery, I often asked myself.

Eventually, Mr. Garland, who was in much debt, relented and said he would take $1,200 for Lizzy and her son.

Shortly after Mr. Garland agreed to give Lizzy her freedom, she married James Keckly.

The day was a happy one, but it faded all too soon. Mr. Keckly—let me speak kindly of his faults—proved dissipated, and a burden instead of a help-mate.

Meanwhile, raising $1,200 proved to be very difficult.

I went to work in earnest to purchase my freedom,
but the years passed and I was still a slave.
Mr. Garland's family claimed so much of my
attention—in fact, I supported them.

Stitch by stitch.

One day, a carriage stopped in front of Lizzy's house.

Mrs. Le Bourgois, one of my kind patrons, got out of it and entered the door. . . . You have many friends in St. Louis and I am going to raise the twelve hundred dollars required among them.

The twelve hundred dollars were raised and at last my son and myself were free. Yes, free! free by the laws of man and the smile of God.

That was November 15, 1855.

It was a time of great tension in the United States. The Northern states and the Southern states had irreconcilable differences and were preparing for war. One of the differences was that the South wanted to keep slavery and the North wanted to abolish it.

Lizzy agreed to receive money from her patrons only under the condition that she would repay them . . . stitch by stitch.

I went to work in earnest, and in a short time paid every cent that was so kindly advanced by my lady patrons of St. Louis.

In the spring of 1860, her debt paid, Lizzy decided to leave St. Louis and move to Washington, D.C.

One of Lizzy's clients was Varina Davis, wife of Senator Jefferson Davis, who would become president of the Confederacy the following year.

At the time of Lizzy's arrival, Washington, D.C., was home to leaders from both sides. Lizzy's beautiful work caught the attention of their wives.

Another client was Mary Anna Custis Lee, wife of Robert E. Lee, the
future commander of the Confederate Army. Mrs. Lee needed a new dress

When Lizzy called on Mrs. Lee, her husband, who was in the room, gave Lizzy one hundred dollars to buy trimmings.

With the money in my pocket, I went out into the street, entered the store of Harper & Mitchell, and asked to look at their laces. When I asked permission to carry the laces to Mrs. Lee, in order to learn whether she could approve my selection or not, he gave a ready assent. When I reminded him that I was a stranger, and that the goods were valuable, he remarked that he was not afraid to trust me—that he believed my face was the index to an honest heart. It was pleasant to be spoken to thus, and I shall never forget the kind words of Mr. Harper.

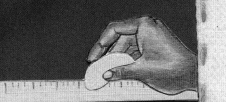

Mrs. Lee's dress was for a party given in honor of the Prince of Wales, and Mrs. Lee had been "in a state bordering on excitement" over what she would wear.

Lizzy began to sew the dress,
stitch by stitch.

Stitch by stitch . . .

The dress was done in time, and it gave complete satisfaction.

Mrs. Lee attracted great attention at the dinner-party, and her elegant dress proved a good card for me. I received numerous orders.

Abraham Lincoln was inaugurated
as the sixteenth president of the
United States on March 4, 1861.
Hearing that Lizzy sewed for
Varina Davis, Mrs. Lincoln was
eager to hire Lizzy too.

*Mrs. L. came forward
and greeted me warmly.
"You have come at last."*

Mrs. Lincoln had purchased bright rose-colored moire-antique fabric and wanted Lizzy to make a dress from it. Lizzy measured Mrs. Lincoln and returned to the White House the next day to fit her.

When Lizzy delivered the dress on the night of the party, Mrs. Lincoln insisted she didn't have enough time and refused to dress and join her guests. Her sister and her cousin were finally able to persuade Mrs. Lincoln to let Lizzy dress her.

Laughing and quoting poetry, the president entered the room, threw himself on the couch, and said,

"I declare, you look charming in that dress. Mrs. Keckly has met with great success."

Mrs. Lincoln's dress was much admired at the party, and Lizzy became the First Lady's regular dressmaker, sewing at least fifteen dresses over the next two seasons . . . stitch by stitch.

The women became friends. They supported each other through times of great tragedy: the death of Lizzy's son George in a Civil War battle, the illness and death of Mrs. Lincoln's son Willie, and the assassination of the president.

More bad times followed as Mary Lincoln became impoverished and outcast. Few people other than Lizzy remained loyal, and eventually the friendship between Mary and Lizzy became strained as well.

Over the years, Lizzy became acquainted with many prominent people. She used her connections to bring awareness to the plight of newly liberated African Americans. In the mid-1800s, approximately ten thousand formerly enslaved men and women had reached the nation's capital. Though they had secured their freedom, many struggled to survive and were forced to live in makeshift camps and tenements. In 1862, Lizzy helped found the Ladies' Contraband Relief Association, which provided food, shelter, and clothing. She served as the association's president and rallied support for their efforts. Lizzy collected contributions from well-to-do African Americans, President Lincoln and the First Lady, and abolitionist luminaries, including Wendell Phillips, Leonard Grimes, and Frederick Douglass.

Lizzy also created opportunities for many African American women. By 1865, she employed almost twenty women in her 12th Street dress shop.

An author as well as a historian, Lizzy wrote a memoir, *Behind the Scenes, or, Thirty Years a Slave, and Four Years in the White House*, published in 1868. She wrote about slavery, the White House, and First Lady Mary Todd Lincoln . . . word by word.

The aftermath proved a great hardship for Lizzy. A reviewer for the *New York Times* criticized the book for "gross violations of confidence," an opinion that was widespread, and upon reading the book, Mary Lincoln ended her friendship with Lizzy.

In 1892, at the age of seventy-four, Lizzy was offered a position as the head of Sewing and Domestic Science Arts at Wilberforce University in Xenia, Ohio. At the university, she continued sewing and teaching young women the same techniques her mother had taught her as a girl.

In the late 1890s Lizzy returned to Washington, D.C., to live in the National Home for Destitute Colored Women and Children, an institution she had helped create. In May 1907, she died in her sleep after an extraordinarily accomplished and compassionate life. Elizabeth Keckly's legacy lives on—in her words, her achievements, her dresses, and in the many stitches of her life's work.

AUTHOR'S NOTE

As a girl growing up in New York, I had never heard of Elizabeth Keckly. We didn't learn about her in school, nor was she mentioned in any of the books I read. It wasn't until I stumbled across her memoir in a bookstore a few years ago that I became familiar with this incredible woman. I felt so inspired by her story, I knew I had to share it with others.

Elizabeth went from being a slave to the First Lady's personal dressmaker. She was a philanthropist, a business owner, and a published author. She not only bought her own freedom and that of her son, she also became a prominent activist. During a time when society tried to silence the voices of African American women, Elizabeth spoke up.

Everything she achieved in her lifetime was done through hard work, resilience, and determination. Although her life was filled with hardship and sadness, Elizabeth never gave up on herself. I wrote *Stitch by Stitch* with the hope that every girl would grow up knowing who Elizabeth Keckly was, and would be as empowered by her story as I have been.

Connie Schofield-Morrison

TIMELINE

1818 Elizabeth Hobbs is born.

1841 Elizabeth's son George is born.

1855 Elizabeth buys her freedom and her son's freedom for $1,200.

1860 Abraham Lincoln is elected president of the United States.

Elizabeth arrives in Washington, D.C., and starts a dressmaking business.

1860–1861 Alabama, Florida, Georgia, Louisiana, Mississippi, South Carolina, and Texas secede from the Union.

1861 Jefferson Davis becomes president of the Confederacy.

Abraham Lincoln is inaugurated.

Elizabeth meets Mary Todd Lincoln.

1861 The Civil War begins.

Elizabeth's son enlists as a white man and dies in battle.

1862 President and Mrs. Lincoln's son Willie dies of typhoid fever.

Elizabeth and members of her church establish the Contraband Relief Association to aid Black refugees.

1864 President Lincoln is reelected.

1865 President Lincoln is inaugurated for his second term.

The Confederacy collapses. The Civil War ends.

President Lincoln is assassinated.

1868 Elizabeth's memoir, *Behind the Scenes, or, Thirty Years a Slave, and Four Years in the White House*, is published.

Mary Todd Lincoln breaks off friendship with Elizabeth as a result of the book.

Elizabeth loses clients in reaction to the book.

1892 Elizabeth takes a faculty position at Wilberforce University in Ohio in the Department of Sewing and Domestic Science Arts.

1907 Elizabeth dies impoverished at the National Home for Destitute Colored Women and Children in Washington, D.C.

BIBLIOGRAPHY

Books

Fleischner, Jennifer. *Mrs. Lincoln and Mrs. Keckly: The Remarkable Story of the Friendship Between a First Lady and a Former Slave*. New York: Broadway Books, 2003.

Keckley, Elizabeth. *Behind the Scenes, or, Thirty Years a Slave, and Four Years in the White House* (version University of North Carolina at Chapel Hill). New York: G. W. Carleton & Co., 1868. Accessed February 28, 2021. https://docsouth.unc.edu/neh/keckley/keckley.html

Periodicals

Sorisio, Carolyn. "Unmasking the Genteel Performer: Elizabeth Keckley's *Behind the Scenes* and the Politics of Public Wrath." *African American Review* 34, no. 1 (2000): 19–38. Accessed February 28, 2021. https://www.jstor.org/stable/2901182?seq=1

Wartik, Nancy. "Overlooked No More: Elizabeth Keckly, Dressmaker and Confidante to Mary Todd Lincoln." *New York Times*, December 12, 2018. Accessed February 25, 2021. https://www.nytimes.com/2018/12/12/obituaries/elizabeth-keckly-overlooked.html

Way, Elizabeth. "The Story of Elizabeth Keckley, Former-Slave-Turned-Mrs. Lincoln's Dressmaker." Interview by Emily Spivack. *Smithsonian Magazine*. Smithsonian Institution, April 24, 2013. Accessed February 25, 2021. https://www.smithsonianmag.com/arts-culture/the-story-of-elizabeth-keckley-former-slave-turned-mrs-lincolns-dressmaker-41112782/

Website Content

Burholt, Eleanor. "Fashion History Timeline, 1818–1907 — Elizabeth Keckley." July 24, 2020. Accessed February 25, 2021. https://fashionhistory.fitnyc.edu/1818-1907-elizabeth-keckley/

Mann, Lina. "From Slavery to the White House: The Extraordinary Life of Elizabeth Keckly." The White House Historical Association. Accessed February 25, 2021. https://www.whitehousehistory.org/from-slavery-to-the-white-house-the-extraordinary-life-of-elizabeth-keckly

Virginia Museum of History and Culture. Accessed March 1, 2021. https://www.virginiahistory.org/collections-and-resources/virginia-history-explorer/elizabeth-keckley

Places to Visit

Burwell School Historic Site. Accessed March 1, 2021. https://www.burwellschool.org

Cultural Tourism DC. Merriweather Home for Children/Elizabeth Keckly, African American Heritage Trail. Accessed February 25, 2021. https://www.culturaltourismdc.org/portal/merriweather-home-for-children/elizabeth-keckly-african-american-heritage-trail

Lefrak, Mikaela. "Historic Downtown Call Boxes Are Now Mini-Museums to Famous Women." October 16, 2019. NPR WNYC. Accessed February 25, 2021. https://www.npr.org/local/305/2019/10/16/770688172/historic-downtown-call-boxes-are-now-mini-museums-to-famous-women

"The Twelve Bronze Statues and Their Stories." Virginia Women's Monument Commission. Accessed February 25, 2021. https://www.womensmonumentcom.virginia.gov/thetwelve.html

To Norma Maccarone, and in memory of Elizabeth Hobbs Keckly
—C.S.M.

For all those who use their craft to light a path out of darkness
—E.Z.

The publisher thanks Jennifer Fleischner, PhD, for her expert review of this book.

Text copyright © 2021 by Connie Schofield-Morrison • Illustrations copyright © 2021 by Elizabeth Zunon • All Rights Reserved
HOLIDAY HOUSE is registered in the U.S. Patent and Trademark Office. • Printed and bound in August 2023 at C&C Offset, Shenzhen, China.
The artwork was created with mixed media including oil paint, paper, fabric, ribbon, embroidery, lace, and appliqué.
www.holidayhouse.com • First hardcover edition published in 2021 • First paperback edition published in 2023
3 5 7 9 10 8 6 4 2

Library of Congress Cataloging-in-Publication Data

Names: Schofield-Morrison, Connie, author. | Zunon, Elizabeth, illustrator. | Title: Stitch by stitch : Elizabeth Hobbs Keckly sews her way to
freedom / by Connie Schofield-Morrison ; illustrated by Elizabeth Zunon. | Other titles: Elizabeth Hobbs Keckly sews her way to freedom
Description: New York : Holiday House, [2021] | Includes bibliographical references. | Audience: Ages 7–10 | Audience: Grades 2–3 | Summary:
"A talented seamstress, born enslaved in 1818, bought freedom for herself and her son"— Provided by publisher. | Identifiers: LCCN 2021007525 (print)
LCCN 2021007526 (ebook) | ISBN 9780823439638 (hardcover) | ISBN 9780823450336 (epub) | Subjects: LCSH: Keckley, Elizabeth,
approximately 1818–1907. | African American women—Biography. | Women slaves—United States—Biography.
Dressmakers—United States—Biography. | Lincoln, Mary Todd, 1818–1882—Relations with African Americans.
Slaves—United States—Biography. | Classification: LCC E457.25 .S36 2021 (print) | LCC E457.25 (ebook) | DDC
306.3/62092 [B]—dc23 | LC record available at https://lccn.loc.gov/2021007525 | LC ebook record available at https://lccn.loc.gov/2021007526

ISBN: 978-0-8234-3963-8 (hardcover)
ISBN: 978-0-8234-5611-6 (paperback)